THE GREAT PHILOSOPHERS

Consulting Editors
Ray Monk and Frederic Raphael

D0148883

SCHOPENHAUER

Michael Tanner

ROUTLEDGE
New York

193
SCH

Published in 1999 by
Routledge
29 West 35th Street
New York, NY 10001

First published in 1997 by
Phoenix
A Division of the Orion Publishing Group Ltd.
Orion House
5 Upper Saint Martin's Lane
London WC2H 9EA

Copyright © 1999 by Michael Tanner.
Printed in the United States of America on acid-free paper.

10 9 8 7 6 5 4 3 2 1

Library of Congress Cataloging-in-Publication Data

Tanner, Michael.
      Schopenhauer / Michael Tanner.
       p. cm.—(The great philosophers : 24)
      Includes bibliographical references.
      ISBN 0-415-92397-2 (pbk.)
      1. Schopenhauer, Arthur, 1788–1860. I. Title. II.
      Series: Great Philosophers   (Routledge (Firm)) : 24.
B3148.T36 1999
193—dc21   99-22482
                                                  CIP

SCHOPENHAUER

Metaphysics and Art

Arthur Schopenhauer (1788–1860) is distinctive among philosophers in the western tradition for holding to a starkly pessimistic view of life, and for emphasizing the will at the expense of the intellect in his portrayal of the mental make-up of man. Indeed it is the second of these two views that leads him to the first, since, as we shall see, he regards the will as something intrinsically evil. And it is because he holds both these views that he comes to give such an important place to the arts in his overall picture of life, and to music in particular. If this sounds like a strange agglomeration of opinions, it is the purpose of this short book to make clear how Schopenhauer manages to combine them.

As he expounds it in his magnum opus, *The World as Will and Representation*, the starting point of Schopenhauer's philosophy is Kant's critical philosophy, as presented in the *Critique of Pure Reason*. Though Schopenhauer disagreed with much that Kant wrote, even in that work, and certainly in the books that Kant wrote subsequently, he espoused some of its key doctrines, and it is necessary to grasp them in order to see how Schopenhauer moved on, as he saw it, from them to his own highly idiosyncratic position. In the Appendix to the first edition of *The World as Will and Representation* (henceforth *WWR*), he subjects the Kantian philosophy to a searching, though by Schopenhauer's standards, respectful critique. What emerges from it, as from the body of *WWR*, is that Schopenhauer from it, as from the body of *WWR*, is that Schopenhauer accepts many of Kant's fundamental positions, while resenting – as most subsequent philosophers have – his elaborate, indeed compulsive architectonic, whereby everything is divided into threes and fours, and categories and concepts are invented merely to satisfy Kant's craving for symmetry.

The starting point of Kant's mature philosophy is a question that he was prompted to ask by the sceptical conclusions of David Hume, who, in Kant's celebrated phrase, awoke him from his dogmatic slumbers. The question is 'How are synthetic *a priori* propositions possible?' What this comes to is this: the statements that we make about ourselves and the world, as a result of experience and observation, are in general *a posteriori*; that is to say, are only made, or rather can only be checked, by seeing how things are. *A priori* propositions, by contrast, can be shown to be true before, or independently of, experience. Such propositions are 'If a man is a bachelor, he is unmarried', which is true by virtue of the meaning of its constituent terms, i.e. by definition. Many philosophers consider that the statements of pure mathematics, which are certainly *a priori*, are also true by virtue of the meaning of the words, numbers and so forth that constitute them. Kant thought differently. He regarded the statement '7 + 5 = 12' as synthetic, and also such statements as 'Every event has a cause.' Although we establish their truth – we realize that they have to be true – without consulting experience, they nevertheless give us genuine information, and not

2

only about the terms or symbols which they are made up of. How can that be?

By itself, that is not a question that arises from anything that Hume thought. What does arise from it is a general doubt about the status of causal laws, and more widely about the way the world is, and how we expect it to continue to be. In Hume's view, we are unable to perceive one event causing another; all we can observe is one event happening immediately after another. We may get so used to sequences of events that we come to attribute necessity to these sequences, but Hume thinks we have no logical right to do that. All we are entitled to say is that when a man has a dose of strychnine, usually he dies. However much we break down the series of events, by dealing, for instance, with atoms rather than observable objects, then with electrons, and so on, we just get more of the same kind of thing: explanation is description at a more basic level. At any given stage in science we take certain elements as fundamental, though subsequent scientists always, at least so far, have gone on to find smaller things. When we get to the stage of atoms, or electrons, or whatever it may be, all we can say is that when one thing happens, another follows. There is never a contradiction in claiming that it won't.

Kant, and many other philosophers, have felt outraged by this conclusion of Hume's. Actually Hume himself was the first person to be upset by it, as he was by many of the conclusions he reached. It led him to abandon the subject, in which he could see no possibility of progress. Kant made his big breakthrough comparatively late in life, effecting

3

what he called his 'Copernican revolution' in philosophy, a view of his achievement which Schopenhauer enthusiastically endorsed. Hume, in common with many philosophers, thought that there is on the one hand nature, including of course human beings, and on the other hand mind, that which understands nature, and which is possessed by human beings and maybe some animals. He believed that nature is independent of the human mind, and that we are in the first place passive in our relation to it. We have imprinted on our minds by way of our sense organs impressions of the external world, and the concepts with which we operate are entirely derived from those impressions. That is the crucial part of what is meant by the term 'empiricism'. This gap between nature and mind is one with disastrous consequences, much of Hume's philosophy being concerned with spelling them out, to his own fascinated horror. We have no guarantee that the world will continue to be as it is now, so our understanding of it is necessarily temporary, and at any moment we might be plunged into incomprehension and chaos.

It was through becoming acquainted with this idea of Hume's, and maybe with the reasons he had for it, that Kant was led to formulate his own mature philosophical views. He realized that if we are not to live in perpetual terror of our understanding of the world suddenly breaking down, we must postulate some relationship between ourselves and the world which ensures that the future will be, in all relevant respects, like the past. His solution to how we might be certain of that is drastic and, in essence, very simple. However, it is extraordinarily elaborate and obscure in detail, partly owing to Kant's addiction to his own newly minted jargon, which Schopenhauer detested. Kant claimed that the framework of experience is supplied not from outside, from the external world itself, but by us. In order for our experience, both of the external world and of ourselves, to be intelligible, it must conform to certain principles (not Kant's word). We have to experience the external world as being in time and space; and we have to experience the contents of that world as being causally related, having persistence through time, and so forth. Kant produced a highly elaborate chain of argument to show that this must be true, and this argument was of a type that has had the greatest influence since. Kant called it 'transcendental': a misleading term, but what it comes to is this. We begin with some undeniable statement, such as that we have sensory experiences. The question then arises of what has to be the case for that statement to be true. That is a transcendental question, and the answer to it gives us the transcendental presuppositions of experience. Kant, as we saw, thought he could demonstrate that objects must exist in space and time, and so forth, and also that in order for us to be able to experience them, we ourselves must be enduring mental substances. And with all this Schopenhauer broadly agreed. He begins *The World as Will and Representation* as follows:

'The world is my representation': this is a truth valid with reference to every living and knowing being, although man alone can bring it into reflective, abstract consciousness. If he really does so, philosophical discernment has dawned on him. It then becomes clear and

5

certain to him that he does not know a sun and an earth, but only an eye that sees a sun, a hand that feels an earth; that the world around him is only a representation, in other words, only in reference to another thing, namely that which represents, and this is himself. If any truth can be expressed *a priori*, it is this; for it is the statement of that form of all possible and conceivable experience, a form that is more general than all others, than time, space, and causality, for all these presuppose it.

Everything that we get to know through the senses, and everything about which we can reason, is ascribed by Kant to what he called the 'phenomenal' world, that is the world of appearance. Our experiences are the result of a collaboration between us and a basic reality of which we can know nothing, except that it must exist. None of the 'categories', or ways in which we experience the world, can be applied to this unknowable reality, not even that it is external or that there is a causal relationship between it and our experiences. This leaves Kant in a more embarrassing situation than he realized. None the less, he felt on the basis of his distinction between the phenomenal and the 'noumenal' world (that is, the world as it is in itself) that he could show that many of the traditional problems of philosophy were unanswerable. Hence the title of his great work, *Critique of Pure Reason*. He wanted, he said, to show what were the limits of reason in order to make way for faith.

That was not an enterprise that appealed to Schopenhauer. Still less appetizing for him was Kant's effort in the

Critique of Practical Reason, his second critique, to show that where pure reason, or what we would normally call simply reason and reasoning, was unable to make any progress, practical reason, which we would normally call moral thought and commitment, could give us what we want and need. For Kant it was obvious that we have to behave in certain ways if we are to be considered as genuine moral agents. And those ways are worked out according to the Categorical Imperative, an unconditional demand made on us. The form of the unconditional demand is: 'Behave in such a way that you can will that the whole of mankind (or even, all rational beings – including angels and God) should behave in the same way.' Kant thought he could demonstrate that this very general precept yielded actual rules of conduct, and forbade others.

Once more, Schopenhauer vehemently disagreed, and the first half of his book *The Two Fundamental Problems of Ethics* (1841) contains a withering attack on Kant's ethics. Elsewhere he attacks the conclusions that Kant draws from them, too. For once more Kant employed his transcendental technique: What has to be the case for there to be moral laws? Alternatively, how are moral laws possible? In the *First Critique* he had shown that pure reason is powerless to deal with the questions that we find most worrying: that is, ones concerned with freedom, personal immortality and the soul, and the existence of God. For our understanding these issues are not only unsettlable but senseless. However, in the *Second Critique* he argues that the presuppositions of morality are that those who obey the moral law should be rewarded, that the world should be a just place. The world in which we take ourselves to be living is manifestly not just. With an insouciance characteristic of philosophers Kant therefore claims that there must be another world – which he identifies as the world in itself, the noumenal world – in which things are as they should be. That means that we must have immortal souls, so that we are suitably treated for our behaviour in this world; and that we are free, despite any appearances that we are merely part of the causal framework of nature; and that, to make sure that things work out as they should, there must be a God who orders them; once more appearances very much to the contrary. This mode of argument, if that is what it can be called, must take the breath away, if one is not familiar with the way in which philosophers help themselves to the conclusions they wish to establish, and then try to think up arguments to support them.

Schopenhauer was certainly scandalized by Kant's proce-dures, which he subjected both to critique and abuse. One of the things that distinguishes Schopenhauer from most other philosophers is his insistence that the world is not the place we would like it to be; and he has no patience with attempts to write off as 'mere appearances' all those elements in life, such as pain, decay, death and the rest of the conditions of existence which Plato and many since have denied, creating a world according to what they fancy. Indeed, Schopenhauer goes to extreme lengths to stress precisely those things that most philosophers have neglected or denied. Philosophy was regarded in the Middle Ages as 'the handmaid of theology', and that is largely what it has continued to be. Even a sceptic such as Hume, who believed neither in immortality nor God, took a generally cheerful view of things, owing to his sunny disposition. However, it is one thing to take a gloomy view of things, as Schopenhauer did; another to offer a fully fledged philosophical justification for it, which he also did. It is, indeed, what constitutes his philosophy, though the metaphysical scaffolding is impressive enough sometimes to conceal what it is the scaffolding for.

In the first book of *WWR* Schopenhauer follows Kant pretty closely. It is the second book, entitled 'The World as Will. First Aspect' that announces his departure from Kant's way of looking at things. He can't accept, as most philosophers have not been able to, Kant's postulation of the phenomenal and the noumenal world. Yet he agrees that with my sense and my reason I do know only the phenomenal world, and that there must be something more than that. How, then, is it possible for me to grasp things as they truly are if I have no privileged mode of access to them? He thinks that in a certain sense we all do, but that it is via a faculty we have that has been widely neglected, at least as conveying information about anything outside itself. The second chapter of Book II begins thus:

> In fact, the meaning that I am looking for of the world that stands before me simply as my representation, or the transition from it as mere representation of the knowing subject to whatever it may be besides this, could never be found if the investigator himself were nothing more than the purely knowing subject (a winged cherub without a body). But he himself is rooted

in that world; and thus he finds himself in it as an *individual;* in other words, his knowledge, which is the conditional supporter of the whole world as representation, is nevertheless given entirely through the medium of a body, and the affections of the body are ... the starting point for the understanding in its perception of this world. For the purely knowing subject as such, this body is a representation like any other, an object among objects. Its movements and actions are so far known to him in just the same way as the changes of all other objects of perception; and they would be equally strange and incomprehensible to him, if their meaning were not unravelled for him in an entirely different way. Otherwise, he would see his own conduct follow on presented motives with the constancy of a law of nature, just as the changes in other objects follow upon causes, stimuli, and motives. But he would be no nearer to understanding the influence of the motives than he is to understanding the connection with its cause of any other effect that appears before him. He would then also call the inner, to him incomprehensible, nature of those manifestations and actions of his body a force, a quality, or a character, just as he pleased, but he would have no further insight into it. All this, however, is not the case; on the contrary, the answer to the riddle is given to the subject of knowledge appearing as individual, and this answer is given in the word *Will.* This and this alone gives him the key to his own phenomenon, reveals to him the significance and shows him the inner mechanism of his being, his actions, his movements. To the subject of knowing, who appears as an individual only through his identity with the body, this body is given in two entirely different ways. It is given in intelligent perception as representation, as an object among others, liable to the laws of these objects. but it is also given in quite a different way, namely as what is known to everyone, and is denoted by the word *will* ... The act of will and the action of the body are not two different states objectively known, connected by the bond of causality; they do not stand in the relation of cause and effect, but are one and the same thing, though given in two entirely different ways, first quite directly, and then in perception for the understanding. The action of the body is nothing but the act of will objectified, i.e., translated into perception.

In other words, in knowing what we will, or rather in willing itself, we have a direct line to what we really are. The action of the body being merely the act of will objectified means that the body itself is the will itself objectified, i.e., translated into perception. So Schopenhauer does not hold, as Kant does, that what is truly real is quite different in kind from anything we experience. On the contrary, it is as beings with urgent desires that we first experience ourselves. Look at a baby lying in its bed and crying for milk or attention; that is Schopenhauer's picture of what we basically are. Our bodies are literally, for him, the phenomenal representation of our wills. And these wills are not subject to the constraint of reason: they are imperious, impatient and, of course, in the first place entirely egoistic.

So far, so good, at least by the standards of metaphysical argument. There is no doubt that the vast majority of previous philosophers had underplayed the role of the will in human life, and had given an over-intellectualized view of our consciousness. Points have often been awarded to Schopenhauer for anticipating Freud, and though it is clearly not the most valuable thing a philosopher can do to put in embryonic terms what a scientist, or pseudo-scientist, is going to say later, it shows a sense of the way things were moving. But clearly problems immediately arise. Can we give any sense to Schopenhauer's claim that the body is the objectification of the will? Is it not because we have a body in the first place that we will things, for instance that we will to have milk, warmth, protection because our bodies, or parts of them, suffer from hunger, cold and exposure? Not to put too fine a point on it, what would the will operate on if the body weren't there for desires concerning it to be generated?

This is only the first stage of Schopenhauer's treatment of the will, however. As the title of his major work suggests, the world in general is to be regarded as Will and Representation. Actually that is rather inaccurate as an indication of what the book states. For Schopenhauer's position is that the world is Will, and appears as Representation. Will has priority, in ontological terms, over Representation. So far we have merely seen that Schopenhauer thinks that we are, in our essence, will. But as his metaphysics develops, it becomes clear that he regards everything that exists as in essence Will. This sounds like, and indeed is, a characteristic piece of metaphysical extravagance. It has led some philosophers, who are in general sympathetic to him but find him going too far here, to suggest that if he had substituted 'energy' for 'will' he would have once more strikingly prefigured the speculations of modern scientists, this time physicists. But if he had wanted to he could have used another word: say, 'force'. As it was, he deliberately used the word 'Will' and stuck with it, one of his later works being entitled *On the Will in Nature* (1836), in which he sought to give examples of the workings of the Will where we wouldn't expect to find them.

What it comes to is that Schopenhauer thought of the Will, the unified cosmic principle that is everything, and underlies all appearances, as unconscious, mindless, therefore only like our own wills in respect of its ruthless urgency. Our wills as we experience them daily when we make an effort to be nice to someone, or to give up smoking, or to satisfy some craving or just an ordinary need, resemble the Will itself only through the sense of lack which looms large in both contexts. Our wills as we ordinarily know them are a highly domesticated affair, as it were. We operate with a full battery of concepts derived from our experience of the empirical world as we perceive it thanks to our sense organs; and with the equipment that we use to make that experience coherent, so that our concepts are a product partly of the way we are, partly of the way the world operates. Thus far Schopenhauer is a good Kantian. But in giving our experience of willing such status he departs radically from Kant, and never returns to

13

him, except in one crucial respect in his aesthetic theory. It is unclear how far Schopenhauer realized that he was transgressing Kantian interdictions in talking about reality when he postulated the Will as what truly exists. For in order to describe it in the enormous amount of detail he does, and with inordinate relish for its ghastliness, he has to rely on concepts that originate in our experience of the world as Representation; and therefore on concepts that really have no business being applied anywhere else. Evidently this is a moot moment in his system, but he presses on, regardless.

Willing something, in our common use of the concept, means willing that there should be some change in the world. We want something that we haven't got, and we take steps to get it, if we don't decide that there are more important considerations militating against getting it, or if we aren't too lazy. In other words, if we were in a state of perfect contentment we wouldn't will anything. That is not contentious. Schopenhauer, however, moves from that, or at any rate this is the effect of his procedure, to argue that since we do will things, we are in a state of perfect discontent. Having quite unthreateningly declared that the thing about ourselves that we are most familiar with is our will, he moves on to the claim that we are all perpetually in a state of extreme dissatisfaction, and that any goals that we achieve are immediately replaced by new desires, so that our condition is incurable. Becoming still more ambitious in his claims, he postulates that the fundamental reason for our state of ineradicable discontent is what he calls the *principium individuationis*, the principle of individuation.

Remembering that the idea of separate things, of individuality in other words, is something that belongs to the world of appearance, and that it can have no grip on the world of ultimate reality, we see that Schopenhauer needs to claim that the idea we have that we are separate from one another is at a deep level an illusion. We are in fact all part of the Primal One, the Will itself, and the individuation that we manifest is something that both guards us from this truth, and gives rise to a great deal of further suffering.

Schopenhauer puts his basic position thus at the end of the second book of *WWR*:

In fact, absence of all aim, of all limits, belongs to the essential nature of the will in itself, which is endless striving … It reveals itself in the simplest form of the lowest grade of the will's objectivity, namely gravitation, the constant striving of which we see, although a final goal for it is obviously impossible. For if, according to its will, all existing matter were united into a lump, then within this lump gravity, ever striving towards the centre, would still always struggle with impenetrability as rigidity or elasticity. Therefore the striving of matter can always be impeded only, never fulfilled or satisfied. But this is precisely the case with the striving of all the will's phenomena. Every attained end is at the same time the beginning of a new course, and so on *ad infinitum*. The plant raises its phenomenon from the seed through stem and leaf to blossom and fruit, which is in its turn only the beginning of a new seed, of a new individual, which once more runs through the old course, and so through endless time. Such also is the life course of the animal; procreation is its highest point, and after this had been attained, the life of the first individual quickly or slowly fades, while a new life guarantees to nature the maintenance of the species, and repeats the same phenomenon ... Eternal becoming, endless flux, belong to the revelation of the essential nature of the will. Finally, the same thing is also seen in human endeavours and desires that buoy us up with the vain hope that their fulfilment is always the final goal of willing. But as soon as they are attained, they no longer look the same, and so are soon forgotten, become antiquated, and are really, although not admittedly, always laid aside as vanished illusions. It is fortunate enough when something to desire and to strive for still remains, so that the game can be kept up of the constant transition from desire to satisfaction, and from that to a fresh desire, the rapid course of which is called happiness, the slow course sorrow, and so that this game may not come to a standstill, showing itself as a fearful, life-destroying boredom, a lifeless longing without a definite object, a deadening languor. According to all this, the will always knows, when knowledge enlightens it, what it wills here and now, but never what it wills in general. Every individual act has a purpose or end; willing as a whole has no end in view.

That is a characteristic specimen of Schopenhauer's prose. He doesn't produce tight or even loose arguments a great deal of the time. Rather he writes incrementally, more or less making the same point but gradually piling on what is usually the agony. He has an anthropomorphic vision of the world, so that for him to say that the lowest grade of the Will's objectivity is gravitation is no metaphor, but a literal truth. His prose has more colour than that of most philosophers; indeed he cultivates a careful literary style, for which we may be grateful at the same time as we need to be vigilant to see that he is not persuading us by mere rhetoric rather than by argument. Note, for instance, in the passage just quoted how he moves from willing at various levels to a claim about willing as a whole, which he says has no object; or alternatively talks of 'the final goal of willing', something most of us don't have in mind and might well find it difficult to recognize. For us having a specific goal in mind and achieving it is at least often a cause of satisfaction. Schopenhauer is trying to persuade us of the futility of willing rather as one might try to persuade someone of the futility of eating by pointing out that however satisfying a given meal may be, it won't be long before another one is needed.

The form of the Will that Schopenhauer is most concerned with is the will-to-live, because it is not only the most pervasive form of the Will with which we come into contact at the level of living things, but it is also the most manifestly irrational. In Volume II of *WWR*, in the chapter called 'Characterization of the Will-to-Live', Schopenhauer writes:

> the human race ... presents itself as puppets that are set in motion by an internal clockwork. For if we compare ... the restless, serious and laborious efforts of men with what they get from them, in fact with what they ever can get, the disproportion becomes apparent, since we

17

recognize that what is to be attained, taken as motive power, is wholly inadequate to explain that movement and that restless activity. Thus, what are a short postponement of death, a small alleviation of need and want, a deferment of pain, a momentary satisfaction of desire, with the frequent and certain victory of death over them all? Taken as actual causes of movement of the human race, what could such advantages achieve? This human race is innumerable through its being constantly renewed; it is incessantly astir, pushes, presses, worries, struggles and performs the whole tragi-comedy of world history. In fact, what says more than anything else, everyone *perseveres* in such a mock existence as long as he possibly can … I have said that those puppets are not pulled from outside, but that each of them bears in itself the clockwork from which its movements result. This is the *will-to-live* manifesting itself as an untiring mechanism, as an irrational impulse, which does not have its sufficient ground or reason in the external world … From the original and uncondi-tioned nature of the will … it is easy to explain that man loves above everything else an existence which is full of want, misery, trouble, pain, anxiety, and then again of boredom, and which, were it pondered over and considered purely objectively, he would of necessity abhor; and that he fears above everything else the end of this existence, which is nonetheless the one and only thing certain for him. Accordingly, we often see a miserable figure, deformed and bent with age, want, and disease, appeal to us from the bottom of his heart for help for the prolongation of an existence, whose end would necessarily appear as altogether desirable, if it was an objective judgement that was the determining factor. Therefore, instead of this, it is the blind will appearing as the tendency to life, the love of life, vital energy; it is the same thing that makes the plants grow.

Schopenhauer's rhetoric is impressive, and has had a very powerful effect on many people, especially artists of various kinds, including most famously Richard Wagner, whose work was revolutionized in several respects by his encounter with *WWR* in 1854. Tolstoy, Thomas Mann, Hardy, Conrad and many, many other writers have found a strong satisfaction in having what they regard as the necessary, inescapable misery of life so lucidly conveyed. And they have found that Schopenhauer's stress on the will is the key to their dissatisfaction, as if what they were hoping for was the performance of an act which meant that they no longer needed to perform any other, yet did not therefore lapse into boredom. For Schopenhauer presents us with a stark choice: either we are dissatisfied, suffering from craving, and stay that way, which is painful. Or we get what we wanted, only to find that we are bored by it. As he writes in Book III:

All *willing* springs from a lack, a deficiency, and thus from suffering. Fulfilment brings this to an end; yet for one wish that is fulfilled there remain at least ten that are denied. Further, desiring lasts a long time, demands and requests go on to infinity; fulfilment is short and is meted out sparingly. But even the final satisfaction itself is only apparent; the wish fulfilled at once makes way for a new one; the former is a known delusion, the latter a delusion not as yet known. No attained object of willing can give a satisfaction that lasts and no longer declines; but it is always like the alms thrown to a begger, which reprieves him today so that his misery may be prolonged until tomorrow ... Essentially it is all the same whether we pursue or flee, fear harm or aspire to enjoyment; care for the constantly demanding will, no matter in what form, continually fills and moves consciousness; but without peace and calm, true well-being is absolutely impossible. Thus the subject of willing is constantly lying on the revolving wheel of Ixion, is always drawing water in the sieve of the Danaids, and is the eternally thirsting Tantalus.

Schopenhauer's tendency to slither from one position to another is more evident here: early on we have 'for one wish that is fulfilled there are at least ten that are denied', but that soon leads to the claim that 'the wish fulfilled ... is a known delusion', a much stronger and not so obviously true position, supposing one does agree with the gloomy first claim.

It is, in fact, an intrinsic part of Schopenhauer's mode of persuasion to be diffuse, which makes quotation difficult. For if he had written with the concision of many philosophers, the questionableness of his drift would be more obvious. As it is, he repeats, with cunning variation, a certain view; then he takes himself to have established, thanks as much to the accretion of examples as by reasoning, a slightly more radical position; and ends up in morose triumph with a much more depressing claim than the one we had originally taken ourselves to be assenting to. Whether one goes along with this dubious procedure is very much a matter of temperament, as indeed much of our agreement or not with philosophical views tends to be. There are many people who gain satisfaction – and they aren't necessarily ones who have had a bad deal from life – from the thought that there is no such thing as genuine fulfilment, even of a temporary kind; or else, like Schopenhauer, they feel that fulfilment is only genuine if it is permanent, a depressingly stringent demand to make.

The idea that life is a matter of ceaseless striving, and that no genuine satisfactions are to be found in it, is of course not new to Schopenhauer. What is new with him is partly his metaphysics of the one Will, underlying all appearances; and partly the analysis of the relationship between the will to achieve something and its fulfilment. For Schopenhauer thought that the so-called pleasure that ensues from gaining an object of desire is nothing more than the temporary cessation of that desire, and maybe the unawareness, for a very brief time, of any other. In the Middle Ages some theologians and philosophers had held to a 'privative' theory of pain or suffering in an attempt to solve the problem of why there is suffering in a world ruled by an omnipotent and all-benevolent deity. This theory maintains that pain and suffering, and correlatively evil, are only the minimum amount of pleasure, which may be nil. Those undesirable states have no positive quality of their own. Schopenhauer holds what we may call a privative theory of pleasure. Hard as it may be to believe, he actually thought that pleasure was nothing more than the absence of pain, that there is no such thing as a genuine feeling of pleasure, either of the localized kind that we associate with bodily satisfactions such as those gained from eating, sexual activity, or being warm. For him there is only the brief absence of hunger, or of the craving for sexual release, or relief from being cold. Furthermore, nature has contrived things so that the asymmetries between pain and pleasure are as tiresome as they can be. Pain, it is often said, is nature's way of telling us that something is wrong; a singularly unhelpful way, often, since it is rarely clear to the person (let alone the animal) that is suffering pain what he should do in order to stop it. Furthermore, pain only occurs, in many cases, when it is too late to do anything about it, so that nature is being merely spiteful, as it were, in informing us that something is incurably wrong with our bodies by means of putting us into fearful agonies. All that is very much on Schopenhauer's side, though he doesn't make as much of it as he might.

One might say that it is inbuilt in the experience of pain that one wants it to stop (the question of masochism, a very interesting one, is not central here, and even advanced masochists only want certain kinds of pain). It would be very useful if it were inbuilt in the experience of pleasure too, at least pleasure of the kind that shows that we have satisfied a bodily need, that the satisfaction has occurred. In general, though, it is not, so we are inclined to over-indulge, thinking that more of what gave us pleasure would give us more; whereas what in fact happens is that we soon stop enjoying a given sensation of pleasure as much as we began by doing, and that we begin to suffer from satiety or nausea or even from disgust. That is also a point Schopenhauer might have made something of. The trouble is that in order to argue it through we have to concede, what in any case should be sufficiently plain, that there is such a phenomenon as positive pleasure; if we don't agree with that, it becomes unintelligible why we should want more of it; indeed there would be no *it* to want more of. We would merely want the temporary cessation of pain to become permanent, which is neither an absurd goal nor one that would lead to harmful consequences. Indeed, for those of us who live in temperate zones, are reasonably well situated and financed, and so forth, the biological demands, or most of them, we have on nature are met: we do not experience thirst and hunger as deprivations. Characteristically we quite enjoy feeling hungry if we know that our hunger is going to be satisfied by a nourishing and pleasant meal, just as thirst is positively pleasurable when there is the immediate prospect of its being quenched.

Schopenhauer has a quick way with this kind of talk, though it is not clear that he can escape from the harm to his view that comes from admitting that we do have positive pleasures. He would say, in fact repeatedly does say, that once our basic needs are satisfied we are in a good position for what Samuel Johnson called 'the hunger of imagination' to get its terrible hold on us. (Although the only reference Schopenhauer makes to Johnson in his chief work is dismissive, their outlooks on life have a great deal in common, especially in the kind of examples they give.) As soon as we are in a position to enjoy ourselves, that is are feeling reasonably comfortable, we fall prey to every kind of anxiety and fear. The body's comfort means that the mind is free to dwell on all the things that could happen to us, an impressive list of horrors. And at the end of it all there is the inevitable fate, which we dread more than anything else, irrational beings that we are. In the second edition of *WWR*, which Schopenhauer published in 1844, and which is more than twice as long as the first edition, he rises to new heights of icy denunciation of our condition, above all, perhaps, in the chapter entitled 'On the Vanity and Suffering of Life'. Here is a characteristic passage:

Everything in life proclaims that earthly happiness is destined to be frustrated, or recognized as an illusion. The grounds for this lie deep in the very nature of things. Accordingly, the lives of most people prove troubled and short. The comparatively happy are often only apparently so, or else, like those of long life, they are rare exceptions; the possibility of these still had to be left, as decoy-birds. Life presents itself as a continual deception, in small matters as well as in great. If it has promised, it does not keep its word, unless to show how little desirable the desired object was; hence we are deluded now by hope, now by what was hoped for. If it has given, it did so in order to take. The enchantment of distance shows us paradises that vanish like optical illusions, when we have allowed ourselves to be fooled by them. Accordingly, happiness lies always in the future, or else in the past, and the present may be compared to a small dark cloud driven by the wind over the sunny plain; in front of and behind the cloud everything is bright, only in itself it casts a shadow. Consequently the present is always inadequate, but the future is uncertain, and the past irrecoverable. With its misfortunes, small, greater, and great, occurring hourly, daily, weekly, and yearly; with its deluded hopes and accidents bringing all calculations to nought, life bears so clearly the stamp of something which ought to disgust us, that it is difficult to conceive how anyone could fail to recognize this, and be persuaded that life is here to be thankfully enjoyed, and that man exists in order to be happy. On the contrary, that continual deception and disillusionment, as well as the general nature of life, present themselves as intended and calculated to awaken the conviction that nothing what-ever is worth our exertions, our efforts, and our strug-gles, and that all good things are empty and fleeting, that the world on all sides is bankrupt, and that life is a business that does not cover the costs; so that our will may turn away from it.

A little further on in the same chapter, Schopenhauer makes his most sustained attack on the nature of our existence:

We feel pain, but not painlessness; care, but not the freedom from care; fear, but not safety and security. We feel desire as we feel hunger and thirst; but as soon as it has been satisfied, it is like the mouthful of food which has been taken, and which ceases to exist for our feelings the moment it is swallowed. We painfully feel the loss of pleasures and enjoyments, as soon as they fail to appear; but when pains cease even after being present for a long time, their absence is not directly felt, but at most they are thought of intentionally by means of reflection. For only pain and want can be felt positively; and therefore they proclaim themselves; well-being, on the contrary, is merely negative. Therefore, we do not become conscious of the three greatest blessings of life as such, namely health, youth and freedom, as long as we possess them, but only after we have lost them; for they too are negations. We notice that certain days of our life were happy only after they have made room for unhappy ones. In proportion as enjoyments and pleasures increase, susceptibility to them decreases; that to which we are accustomed is no longer felt as a pleasure. But in precisely this way is the susceptibility to suffering increased; for the cessation of that to which we are accustomed is felt painfully. Thus the measure of what is necessary increases through possession, and thereby the capacity to feel pain. The hours pass the more quickly the more pleasantly they are spent, since pain, not pleasure, is the positive thing, whose presence makes itself felt. In just the same way we become conscious of time when we are bored, not when we are amused. Both cases prove that our existence is happiest when we perceive it least; from this it follows that it would be better not to have it. Great and animated delight can be positively conceived only as the conse-quence of great misery that has preceded it; for nothing can be added to a state of permanent contentment except some amusement or even the satisfaction of vanity. Therefore, all poets are obliged to bring their heroes into painful and anxious situations, in order to be able to liberate them again from them. Accordingly dramas and epics generally describe only fighting, suffering, tormented men and women, and every work of fiction is a peep-show in which we observe the spasms and convulsions of the agonized human heart.

It is worth looking at this last passage a little more closely, for it is so typical of the way in which Schopenhauer proceeds. The general level of his remarks is that of statements about the universal condition of humanity, founded on observation. More than most philosophers, he makes frequent reference to particular phenomena in order to show that he knows what he is talking about. Yet if many of his statements can be construed either as empirical generalizations, or as conceptual truths about the nature of pain, pleasure, time and so forth, it is unclear what evidence we would have to produce in order to refute them. The claim that 'well-being is merely negative', which we have seen is so fundamental to Schopenhauer's *Weltanschauung*, is just stated. Since it seems strongly counterintuitive, one would like him to justify it, but he hurries on. Indeed, one could say that Schopenhauer's prose style discourages close attention; he lures one, by his very sentence construction, into moving along with him without close attention to individual sentences. Take the statement that 'We do not become conscious of the three greatest blessings of life as such, namely health, youth and freedom, as long as we possess them.' That is something that is often true, but by no means invariably. We are, if we are surrounded by sick people, often highly aware of our privileged state; a young person may be enviously reminded by an older one of the advantages of youth, especially in a youth-oriented culture such as our own, and may warmly agree about his position, and make the best of it; and certainly it is characteristic of people in our own century to rejoice in their freedom, when it has been possible to appreciate with such immediacy the bondage of a huge proportion of mankind. So though we may agree with Schopenhauer that people are often negligent of their good fortune until it has deserted them, this is more of the registering of a tendency than the statement of a universal truth, and it certainly is not a necessary or conceptual truth.

He becomes still more extravagant when he claims that health, youth and freedom are 'negations'. If that means that health is the absence of illness, etc., then we can only reply that one might better say that illness is the absence of health. And between youth and old age, it is very hard to see why one should be considered the positive and the other the negative condition, or even that a claim to either effect would make any sense. We may freely admit that time spent pleasantly goes unnoticed, while when we are bored we are conscious of little other than time. We may even admit that it is the bad things in life that are more conspicuous than the good ones. In George Eliot's *Daniel Deronda*, when Gwendolen Harleth is proposed to by Grandcourt, and he says, 'You shall have whatever you like,' she replies, 'And nothing that I don't like – please say that, because I think I dislike what I don't like more than I like what I like,' George Eliot adds, 'said Gwendolen, finding herself in the woman's paradise where all her nonsense is adorable'. But for Schopenhauer – and surely he is accurate here – we all feel as Gwendolen does. Acute pain is more painful, as it were, than acute pleasure is pleasurable. That at least is true on the somatic level. When we move to the consideration of happiness, things may be more complicated, but then in Schopenhauer's view happiness is either delusive or else to be achieved only by very special disciplines and procedures, which result in a state that may be better characterized by some word other than 'happiness'.

If Schopenhauer were a thoroughgoing pessimist, he would leave things there. And if the term 'pessimism' means the view that this is the worst of all possible worlds, or something like that, then it is a grave mistake for Schopenhauer to be called a pessimist, since he thinks that life can be ameliorated in several ways, most of them of a highly traditional kind, though he puts them to somewhat unconventional use, since he is working from a position unlike that of other philosophers, at least western ones. He also shuns the obvious conclusion that one might draw from accepting the truth of the various passages I have quoted claiming to prove the appallingness, the necessary ghastliness, of existence. That, one might think, would be suicide. Schopenhauer is resolutely opposed to such an idea, turning away from it with the revulsion that shows how much of traditional Christian morality survives in his outlook. Unlike the Romans, whom in many respects he admired, and who regarded choosing the moment of one's death as nobler than waiting for it to happen, he seems to think that we should go on living as long as we can, very much as Christians who regard this world as a vale of tears still postpone their departure from it as long as possible. For Schopenhauer thinks that the denial of the will to live is the only way to reach quietus; otherwise we are subject to rebirth, a matter on which he remains vague, but seems seriously to believe in. But he claims that:

> Far from being denial of the will, suicide is a phenomenon of the will's strong affirmation. For denial has its essential nature in the fact that the pleasures of life, not its sorrows, are shunned. The suicide wills life, and is dissatisfied merely with the conditions on which it has come to him. Therefore he by no means gives up the will-to-live, but merely life, since he destroys the individual phenomenon ... Thus the will-to-live appears just as much in this suicide as in the ease and comfort of self-preservation, and the sensual pleasure of procreation ... The suicide denies merely the individual, not the species. We have already found that, since life is always certain to the will-to-live, and suffering is essential to life, suicide, or the arbitrary destruction of an individual phenomenon, is a quite futile and foolish act, for the thing-in-itself remains unaffected by it.

Admittedly this passage, and the other ones in which he discusses the topic, depend on Schopenhauer's metaphysical views; if we were as separate from one another as we think we are normally, then his argument would carry no conviction at all. As it is, one can't help feeling that his traditional Christian-type view of suicide has led him to take this hostile line about it. The motives of the would-be suicide would hardly seem to be a decisive factor in determining whether he was right or wrong to perform the act. If he had high expectations of life, and found that it is as wretched as Schopenhauer says, then it would seem natural for him to put an end to an existence which, he is assured, will not improve.

Or will it? We come now to the crux of Schopenhauer's moral teaching, the recipes that he provides for making life more tolerable than his many gloomy accounts suggest that it ever could be. Throughout our consideration of them, we must remember that it is the will that is the driving force, the pervasive factor, and that therefore, since it is the source of all pain, somehow it has to be denied. Yet if there is truly, at the deepest level, nothing but the will, the question arises, and doesn't go away, of how the will can negate itself. However, we will first look at some of the ways that Schopenhauer recommends we try.

Unlike the vast majority of philosophers, he assigns to the arts a central role in his system. It isn't just that he gives a more detailed account of them than most western philosophers have; he builds them into his total system as an integral part. This is made possible for him by a further resort to Kant. In the *Critique of Judgment* Kant assigns to what he calls judgements of taste, which may be of nature or of art, a peculiar quality: disinterestedness. By that he means something that can only be explained by reference to the rest of his system. For Kant, when we are behaving as phenomenal beings in the world of appearance, we take an interested attitude to things in the sense that we have one or another kind of design on them, we use them and view them with an eye to seeing what their function might be. And when we are acting morally, that is when our noumenal, or as Kant and Schopenhauer quaintly call it our 'intelligible', self is acting, it is still with the purpose of doing good or right things. For Kant in general our lives are played out as dramas of desire and duty, and for most of the time we are only concerned with things insofar as they are part of that drama. But it is possible to take an aesthetic interest in them; that is, not to see them as performing any kind of role, but just as objects to be enjoyed for themselves. They might be thought to be providing a kind of relaxation for us, but in fact Kant employs aesthetic experiences to fulfil a vital function in his system, which otherwise might fall apart. He wants to use our experiences of the beautiful, and of the sublime – the two usual eighteenth-century categories – to bring together the two otherwise quite separate, and, it would appear, irreconcilable modes of existence, the phenomenal and the noumenal.

Schopenhauer's problem is a quite different one, though it is as acute as Kant's. However, he presents aesthetic experience in very much the same terms, and with elaborate tribute to Kant. He really does seek peace in contemplation of beauty, and finds it through that same – or at any rate very closely similar – lack of interest (in the appropriate sense) that Kant had discerned. He takes a somewhat different route, however. For reasons that none of his commentators finds it easy to grasp, Schopenhauer introduces into his system the Platonic Ideas. He takes them to be the highest grade of objectification of the will. Lower down the scale are various kinds of individual thing. But when we arrive at Platonic Ideas, then 'not themselves entering into time and space, the medium of individual, they remain fixed, subject to no change, always being, never having become. The particular things, however, arise and pass away; they are always becoming and never are.' As with Plato, one understands as long as one doesn't probe too closely what Schopenhauer is saying. There is a crucial difference, though. For Plato the Ideas are also ideal, in the sense that they are perfect, while everything below, i.e., in space and time, is imperfect, at best an imitation of them. For Schopenhauer, by contrast, what things as we know them phenomenally are is bad, not because they are imperfect imitations of what is good, but because the ultimate nature of things, the Will, is itself the source of all pain. It seems to follow – a conclusion that Schopenhauer strangely never draws – that the Ideas must be, as it were, ideally bad. It is therefore wholly puzzling how an intimate relationship with them could prove valuable or pleasurable. Yet that is what Schopenhauer claims.

Part of his answer, supposing that he is aware of the problem, would seem to lie in the whole complex of the aesthetic situation. For Schopenhauer writes:

In the aesthetic method of consideration we found *two inseparable constituent parts*: namely, knowledge of the subject not as an individual thing, but as Platonic *Idea*, in other words, as persistent form of this whole species of things; and the self-consciousness of the knower, not as individual, but as *pure, will-less subject of knowledge*. The condition under which the two constituent parts appear always united was the abandonment of the method of knowledge that is bound by the principle of sufficient reason, a knowledge that, on the contrary, is the only appropriate kind for serving the will and also for science.

Then Schopenhauer embarks on one of his agonizing accounts of willing, already quoted. The paragraph that follows registers the contrast:

When an external cause or inward disposition suddenly raises us up out of the endless stream of willing, and snatches knowledge from the thraldom of the will, the attention is now no longer directed to the motives of willing, but comprehends things free from their relation to the will. Thus it considers things without interest, without subjectivity, purely objectively; it is entirely given up to them in so far as they are merely representations, and not motives. Then all at once the peace, always sought but always escaping us on that first path of willing, comes to us of its own accord, and all is well with us. It is the painless state, prized by Epicurus as the highest good and as the state of the gods; for that moment we are delivered from the miserable pressure of the will. We celebrate the Sabbath of the penal servitude of willing; the wheel of Ixion stands still.

Schopenhauer is, as we have already seen, rather keen on the wheel of Ixion. It needs, however, another condition fulfilled before we are free of it. Schopenhauer adds:

But this is just the idea that I described as necessary for

knowledge of the Idea, as pure contemplation, absorption in perception, being lost in the object, forgetting all individuality, abolishing the kind of knowledge which follows the principle of sufficient reason, and comprehends only relations. It is the state where, simultaneously and inseparably, the perceived individual thing is raised to the Idea of its species, and the knowing individual to the pure subject of will-less knowing, and now the two, as such, no longer stand in the stream of time and all other relations. It is then all the same whether we see the setting sun from a prison or from a palace.

So what is clear is that Schopenhauer connects the state of will-lessness with contemplation of the Idea, as if it would hardly be possible in relation to particular things.

One wonders whether he went in for introspection before he put this view forward. For if he did, it would be interesting to know what contemplation of the Idea is like. The questions that have always beset Plato's account – in contemplating the perfect bed, would it be double or single, a four-poster or a camp bed, etc.? – arise in just the same way for Schopenhauer. And if there were the perfect Idea of each kind of bed, that would land us with something quite close to a reduplication of the physical world. It is not clear why the state of will-less contemplation should need to be of Ideas rather than of individual things. Would one recognize the contemplation of an Idea if one were confronted with it? We can, of course, contemplate concepts, such as justice, even chairhood; and we can contemplate such abstract entities as numbers, though not without the help of numerals. How, though, would we contemplate

35

an Idea by gazing at a Dutch still life? Schopenhauer seems to go some way towards refuting himself when he writes:

> Inward disposition, predominance of knowing over willing, can bring about this state in any environment. This is shown by those admirable Dutchmen who directed such purely objective perception to the most insignificant objects, and set up a lasting monument of their objectivity and spiritual peace in paintings of *still life*.

It would be widely claimed that the mysterious beauty of many Dutch paintings is a matter of their superb portrayal of the intense individuality of those insignificant objects. Certainly one feels in intense relationship with a particular thing rather than a class of things, or the Idea of a thing, whatever that might turn out to be. I suspect that Schopenhauer went down this unprofitable path because he thought that knowledge was of the universal rather than of the particular; a view that many philosophers have held. Particular objects, in their materiality and specificity, have often been felt to be lacking in the dignity which knowledge bestows, or which is bestowed on knowledge. Alternatively, he might have been motivated by the Aristotelian view that art in general, or tragedy in particular, is more philosophical than history because it deals in univeral truths. Why, it has often been wondered, should we be interested in a particular thing if we can't extrapolate from it? It is a good question, and the idea that art, like philosophy, deals with recurring elements in experience has been very tenacious.

That is a different matter, though, from claiming that art deals with Platonic Ideas. Either they turn out to be the same as concepts, in which case the claim is not interesting; or they are something drastically different, which has normally been the suggestion, in which case we would like to know what they are. What Schopenhauer says on the subject is uncharacteristically obscure:

> The *Idea* is the unity that has fallen into plurality by virtue of the temporal and spatial form of our intuitive apprehension. The *concept*, on the other hand, is the unity once more produced out of plurality by means of abstraction through our faculty of reason ... It follows from all that has been said that the concept, useful as it is in life, serviceable, necessary, and productive as it is in science, is eternally barren and unproductive in art.

Such is Schopenhauer's reverence for Plato that he seems to feel no need to do anything more than invoke his name, as though the extreme obscurity of his view on this subject, among others, needed no clarification. What makes it more odd is the extreme difference in their overall metaphysics, even if they both contrive to be monists of a sort, in the end. Plato seems to identify the final forms of the Good, the Beautiful and the True; Schopenhauer suggests no such identification, but he does have the primal, ultimately undifferentiated Will, so that it is still more difficult to see how he can espouse the cause of the Ideas, since they are of things that, to the extent that they are separate, must be to some extent delusive.

Schopenhauer, like Kant in his *Third Critique*, makes a good deal of the idea of *genius*.

> Only through pure contemplation, which becomes entirely absorbed in its object, are the Ideas comprehended. And the nature of *genius* consists precisely in the pre-eminent ability for such contemplation. Now as this demands a complete forgetting of our own person and of its relations and connections, the *gift of genius* is nothing but the most complete *objectivity*, i.e., the objective tendency of the mind, as opposed to the subjective directed to our own person, i.e., to the will. Accordingly, genius is the capacity to remain in a state of pure perception, to lose oneself in perception, to remove from the service of the will the knowledge which originally existed only for this service. In other words, genius is the ability to leave entirely out of sight our own interest, our willing, and our aims, and consequently to discard entirely our own personality for a time, in order to remain *pure knowing subject*, the clear eye of the world.

This is worth quoting at some length because it adumbrates Schopenhauer's view of the saint as well as of the artist. When he talks of the genius he means specifically the artist, but he might equally well mean the scientist, at least the one who has no eye on the purposes to which his research might be put. To that extent perhaps he is effecting, after all, some kind of quasi-Platonic merger between the Beautiful (artist), the Good (saint) and the True (scientist). There are hints that he thinks that, but if he had thought it through clearly he would, in line with his usual practice, have celebrated his achievement at greater length. He does make clear in this passage how he takes the will to operate in a selfish, subjective way on particular objects, while knowledge tends towards the disinterested, the objective and the universal. This is in line with the traditional prejudices of philosophers, so much to that none of them seems to feel the need to defend it. Schopenhauer further seems unable to conceive of a function for art which is not either volitional or cognitive. In particular, the emotions get short shrift, perhaps because they are considered merely manifestations or implements of the will. The idea that art might be expressive is not one that Schopenhauer entertains.

What does seem odd is that art, in so far as it has so many things going for it, is approved by Schopenhauer when it is so likely to detain us in this world. For Schopenhauer is not inclined to break the traditional connection between aesthetic experience and pleasure, and to that extent, since the pleasure must be of a rare order not simply to be discounted as delusive, he seems to be endorsing an activity which many people have taken to justify living; though as an explicit doctrine that post-dated Schopenhauer. A person who manages, for much of the time, to engage in disinterested contemplation is one for whom life must be quite attractive. One might take as an example Schopenhauer himself, though he was admittedly contemplating how dreadful life is. But then since that is the truth, the most fundamental truth there is, how could anyone be exhilarated by it? But if no one should be, then the cognitive function of art is once more called into question. I don't want to press the issue too hard, since in some ways Schopenhauer is only in the same position as everyone who is confronted by the question of why they enjoy witnessing suffering, listening to the expression of painful emotions, and so forth. But where it has been usual to see a problem there, and everyone since Aristotle has had a go at dealing with it, if they have been concerned with response to the arts at all, Schopenhauer seems to be unaware that he needs to say something. Replacing specific things and willing with the Ideas and knowledge appears to him to elucidate the value of art conclusively.

When Schopenhauer gets on to the specific art forms, he has many shrewd things to say, and many questionable ones. He begins with architecture, moves on to sculpture and historical painting, goes on at great but justified length about human beauty and its representation, has an especially striking section on the Laocoon and on Lessing's treatise on it and the issues it gives rise to; and also is original and convincing on the nude in sculpture. He discusses allegory and symbolism with a knowledge of examples welcome among philosophers. There is a long discussion of lyric poetry, then, as one would expect, Schopenhauer presents his theory of tragedy. Here he gives the lead to Nietzsche for *The Birth of Tragedy*, a book striking for its lack of quotations from writers Nietzsche admired, apart from a huge one from *WWR*, though Schopenhauer is far less speculative. His central thesis is that

[the will] reaches the point where the phenomenon, the

veil of Maya, no longer deceives it. It sees through the form of the phenomenon, the *principium individuationis*; the egoism resting on this expires with it. The *motives* that were previously so powerful now lose their force, and instead of them, the complete knowledge of the real nature of the world, acting as a *quieter* of the will, produces resignation, the giving up not merely of life, but of the whole will-to-live itself. Thus we see in tragedy the noblest men, after a long conflict and suffering, finally renounce for ever all the pleasures of life and the aims till then pursued so keenly, or cheerfully and willingly give up life itself.

Schopenhauer then catalogues the various ways in which great misfortune can be presented by the tragic poet. That rounds off his treatment of the various arts, except for the last.

He gets under way with obvious excitement.

We began with architecture, whose aim as such is to elucidate the objectification of the will at the lowest grade of its visibility, where it shows itself as the dumb striving of the mass, devoid of knowledge and conforming to law; yet it already reveals discord with itself and conflict, namely that between gravity and rigidity. Our observations ended with tragedy, which presents us in terrible magnitude and distinctness at the highest grade of the will's objectification that very conflict of the will with itself. After this, we find that there is yet another fine art that remains excluded, and was bound to be excluded, from our consideration, for in the systematic

41

> connection of our discussion there was no fitting place
> for it; this art was *music*. It stands quite apart from all the
> others. In it we do not recognize the copy, the
> repetition, of any Idea of the inner nature of the world.

Schopenhauer has put his finger on something about music which almost all serious music lovers are often puzzled by, and remain, usually, at a loss to explain. On the one hand music seems to be – at least this applies to purely instrumental music, which as a large-scale affair was a relatively new phenomenon in the West, less than two centuries old as a major art-form when Schopenhauer wrote about it – a self-sufficient series of sounds, which succeed one another according to 'laws' which bear only tenuous analogies to anything outside music. In this way it is like chess, another extremely elaborate activity that seems capable of endless expansion, but one that is autonomous, its rules bearing some relationship to the rules of armed or other combat; but that is as far as it goes. Music also bears an analogy to mathematics; it is striking how many people who are good at one of these three compelling pursuits are also good at, or take a very strong interest in, the others. Mathematics is especially fascinating, and an exasperating topic for philosophers, since it both proceeds according to its own laws, as does chess; but it also works wonderfully well, for the most part, in application to experience. It even seems that physicists can work out in sets of equations predictions or explanations about the behaviour of the whole universe. It is that kind of correspondence that makes a Kantian account of the relationship between us and the world tempting.

In the case of music philosophers have, on the whole, shown a notable lack of interest. That is partly because most of them seem to have little appetite for music, a fact to be noted rather than pondered. Schopenhauer is one of the great exceptions, Nietzsche and Wittgenstein being two of the others; Nietzsche's philosophy always has music in at least the background, and Wittgenstein certainly thought of music as a deep phenomenon, though he wrote little about it that is valuable. It is Schopenhauer alone who gives music a hugely important position in his system, seeing it as perhaps the most important of human activities, though whether he should therefore look as favourably on it is a question, given his overall account of the worthlessness such strenuous exertions as composing must involve.

Having set up his position about the key role of music, Schopenhauer then goes on to make himself clearer.

> It is such a great and exceedingly fine art, its effect on man's innermost nature is so powerful, and it is so completely and profoundly understood by him in his innermost being as an entirely universal language, whose distinctness surpasses even that of the world of perception itself, that in it we certainly have to look for more than that 'unconscious exercise in arithmetic in which the mind does not know that it is counting' (Leibniz, *Letters*). Yet he was quite right, in so far as he considered only its immediate and outward significance, its exterior. But if it were nothing more, the satisfaction afforded by it would inevitably be similar to that which we feel when a sum in arithmetic comes out right, and could not be that profound pleasure with which we see

the deepest recesses of our nature find expression. Therefore, from our standpoint where the aesthetic effect is the thing we have in mind, we must attribute to music a far more serious and profound significance that refers to the innermost being of the world and of our own self. In this regard the numerical ratios into which it can be resolved are related not as the thing signified, but only as the sign. That in some sense music must be related to the world as the depiction to the thing depicted, as the copy to the original, we can infer from the analogy with the remaining arts, to all of which this character is peculiar; from their effect on us, it can be inferred that that of music is on the whole of the same nature, only stronger, more rapid, more necessary and infallible. Further, its imitative reference to the world must be very profound, infinitely true, and really striking, since it is instantly understood by everyone ... Yet the point of comparison between music and the world, the regard in which it stands to the world as a copy or a repetition, is very obscure.

It is here that Schopenhauer is able to make his great leap in his claims for music, thanks to the metaphysical system that he has created, and which might be felt to have been constructed for the sake of putting music at its climax; though in fact Schopenhauer goes on to offer further recipes for salvation from the omnipresent tyranny of the will-to-live. But Schopenhauer doesn't think he can prove his claims, only that they will find a convinced response in the sympathetic reader. He writes:

This explanation [which he is about to provide] is quite sufficient for me, and satisfactory for my investigation, and will be just as illuminating also to the man who has followed me thus far, and has agreed with my view of the world. I recognize, however, that it is impossible to demonstrate this explanation, for it assumes and establishes a relation of music as a representation to that which of its essence can never be representation, and claims to regard music as the copy of an original that can itself never be directly represented. I must leave the acceptance or denial of my view to the effect that both music and the whole thought communicated in this work have on the reader.

It is a credit to Schopenhauer that he treads so carefully here, since he is on treacherous ground, though no more treacherous than quite a lot of other ground over which he has unguardedly moved.

He goes on immediately:

The (Platonic) Ideas are the adequate objectification of the will. To stimulate the knowledge of these by depicting individual things (for works of art themselves are always such) is the aim of all the other arts. Hence all of them objectify the will only indirectly, in other words, by means of the Ideas. As our world is nothing but the phenomenon or appearance of the Ideas in plurality through entrance into the *principium individuationis* (the form of knowledge possible to the individual as such), music, since it passes over the Ideas, is also quite independent of the phenomenal world, positively ignores it, and, to a certain extent, could still exist even if there were no world at all, which can not be said of the other arts. Thus music is as *immediate* an objectification and copy of the whole *will* as the world itself, indeed as the Ideas are, the multiplied phenomenon of which constitutes the world of individual things. Therefore music is by no means like the other arts, namely a copy of the Ideas, but *a copy of the will itself*, the objectivity of which are the Ideas. For this reason the effect of music is so very much more powerful and penetrating than is that of the other arts, for these others speak only of the shadow, but music of the essence.

For anyone who, like Schopenhauer, feels that music is incomparably the most powerful and the most important of the arts, this account is attractive, even if one can't accept his metaphysics. For music does, at its finest, for example in Bach's *48 Preludes and Fugues* or Beethoven's late string quartets – Schopenhauer is oddly undiscriminating about it – seem to express something that is deeper than the other arts. Whether we can explain this other than by elaborating a full-scale metaphysic into which it fits is a moot point. Nietzsche was later to dismiss his own early, heavily Schopenhauer-influenced *The Birth of Tragedy* as 'artist's metaphysics', and if he meant by that metaphysics spun out for the sake of glorifying art, or in his case a particular art-form, one sympathizes with his contempt, at the same time as one feels how such an incredible phenomenon as music could lead one along that path.

The question that Schopenhauer once more ducks is why we should value music so highly if it does what he says. For granted his many lurid descriptions of the will, as we have seen some of them, why should it be the glory of an art-form that it serves as what Nietzsche was to call 'a telephone to the infinite', when the infinite is so undesirable? There has been a long tradition in western thinking about art to the effect that the more closely it approaches a copy of the truly real, the greater it is. That, however, is only a theory one might wish to hold if the truly real is in itself something desirable; as in western philosophy it almost always has been. Since it is Schopenhauer's distinction to find the truly real appalling, it is all the stranger that he should hymn the virtues of an art-form that is in such direct contact with it. It is as if he had unthinkingly taken over certain assumptions of the tradition that he was otherwise at great pains to negate. We find the same inadvertence, as it were, in parts of his ethical thinking. One would have suspected, *a priori*, that if music is as wonderful as Schopenhauer says it is, that must be because it puts the maximum gulf between itself and the will. This tiresome need of art to be 'truthful', when the truth is disgusting, is what Nietzsche only came to free himself from – granted his general outlook – late in life when he wrote (and then only in a notebook): 'We have art in order that we may not perish of the truth. Truth is *ugly*.' Why didn't Schopenhauer say the same?

I conjecture, before continuing to expound him, that he may have had some view of art as managing to avenge us by presenting the world in a more truthful way than anything else, and yet at the same time putting it in its place, so that we could actually find it beautiful, or

47

otherwise revel in it. Just as Thomas Mann, a great admirer of Schopenhauer, wrote that in his prose 'we feel ourselves avenged by the heroic word', so we might feel that we are avenged by the heroic tones of music. Yet that won't really do. For we are moved to ecstasy by music, elevated and even transfigured in a way that is inconceivable if we are to stick to Schopenhauer's account.

When he becomes more detailed, Schopenhauer again only reinforces our sense that he ought not to be celebrating what he is discussing. For he writes:

Music does not express this or that particular and definite pleasure, this or that affliction, pain, sorrow, horror, gaiety, merriment or peace of mind, but joy, pain, sorrow, horror, gaiety, merriment, peace of mind *themselves*, to a certain extent in the abstract, their essential nature, without any accessories, and so also without the motives for them. Nevertheless, we understand them perfectly in this abstracted quintessence. Hence it arises that our imagination is so easily stirred by music, and tries to shape that invisible, yet vividly aroused, spirit-world that speaks to us directly, to clothe it with flesh and bone, and thus to embody it in an analogous example. This is the origin of the song with words, and finally of the opera ... It is just this universality which belongs uniquely to music, together with the more precise distinctness, that gives it that high value as the panacea of all our sorrows. Therefore, if music tries to stick too closely to the words, and to mould itself according to the events, it is endeavouring to speak a language not its own. No one has kept so free from this mistake as Rossini; hence his music speaks its *own* language so distinctly and purely that it requires no words at all, and therefore produces its full effect even when rendered by instruments alone.

Once again we can see why Schopenhauer has gone down so well with philosophically inclined music lovers. Yet surely, again, if music fulfils these purposes so delightfully, it can only induce us to think that life is worth living, or at any rate worth hanging on to, once we have committed what Schopenhauer curiously calls the 'original sin' of being born. Furthermore, it becomes obscure how, in doing what he says it does, that is, in expressing the emotions in themselves, free of the circumstances that give rise to them, music is either doing something that we should prize, granted that it is intelligible, or that it is really a copy of the will itself. This will, underlying all phenomena, is unknowable by concepts, which – as Schopenhauer agrees with Kant – are applicable to phenomena only. It is therefore not amenable to being characterized by gaiety, merriment, pain, sorrow, and so forth. Schopenhauer makes the mistake here of thinking that if we abstract these feelings from their objects, we shall have a deeper understanding of them. He is thus doubly confused. To deal with the latter point first: he seems to think, as many philosophers have done, that emotions are inner states which are recognizable purely by introspection: we see how we are feeling, and know what emotions we are having. But at least for many emotions it makes no sense to say that one is experiencing them apart from a specific context. That is obviously the case with such emotions as jealousy; one couldn't conceivably introspect and discover that it was jealousy one was feeling, and then cast about to see what the object of the jealousy was. There are, of course, confusions we can have about such states, discovering that while we thought we were jealous of A on account of B, in fact we are jealous of B on account of A. Similarly, we might mislocate the object of our pride. We need to spend a lot of time telling ourselves the truth about our emotional lives. But from the fact that we make mistakes concerning what or whom we are feeling about, it certainly doesn't follow that the ideal thing would be to have emotions without any objects. And – to reiterate the first point – Schopenhauer simply is not entitled to use our concepts for the emotions we have in the phenomenal world to characterize what we feel (if he is even entitled to the concept of feeling) in the noumenal world.

In fact, Schopenhauer's general philosophy commits him to saying that the fewer feelings we have, the better, with some rather rare exceptions. In this he is like Spinoza, though less refined. And no doubt the life of feeling is closely and inextricably involved with the surging, ineluctable will, which is a bad thing on this view. But if the implication is that the will is constituted partly by emotions which are looking for objects, then that is only intelligible for some emotions, and in any case they presuppose the reality of separate objects, which is to say the *principium individuationis*, the source of so much of our woe. If the will is a unity, only deludedly thought by us to be broken up into separable people and other natural objects, then many emotions are entirely based on that false view we have of the world, and so to posit our experience of music as experience of the will itself is clearly mistaken. The will itself, in its state of undifferentiatedness, could not be envious, grateful, or even – to take examples that are genuinely harmful to Schopenhauer's ethics – malicious or egoistic or compassionate. For any of these last three states, constituted as they are partly of emotions and partly of patterns of behaviour, rely on the delusion of separateness. So just as Schopenhauer's ethics, which postulates these three basic drives in man, is dealing with life only as phenomenon, so his aesthetics of music, in so far as the stress moves to the expression of emotions which we only experience because we believe that we are individuals, is adequate, if at all, to the world of appearance.

It is very hard to know, in fact, what the undifferentiated world might feel. Nietzsche characterizes it, in *The Birth of Tragedy*, as a primal swirl of pain-cum-pleasure, and though even that may be too specific, it seems wise to leave it at that. That means, however, that the way in which we usually appreciate music, when we are concerned with it from the point of view of emotional expression, is something that we value because it, at best, takes us into the deepest recesses of our empirical selves, the selves which maintain a constant attempt to remain sharply individuated. So whatever the truth about music, how and even if it is expressive, it can't be expressive of ultimate reality. Nor, to hammer the point home, is it easy to see how if it were it would be such a wonderful thing. Art can transfigure the commonplace, as in much Dutch painting; it can render the intolerable tolerable, as sometimes seems to be the case with tragedy. What it is hard to conceive of it doing is expressing or copying (Schopenhauer is offhand with his terminology here) the will itself.

It is significant that Schopenhauer liked Rossini so much. Though he doesn't enlarge on the praise that he gives him in passing in the last quotation, one might conjecture that the reasons he enjoyed him may have been multiple. It is hard to dismiss the suspicion that the ubiquity of malice in Rossini's comic operas would have gone down very well with the great misanthropist that Schopenhauer was. But more germane to his central thesis than that, the claim Schopenhauer makes that Rossini's music speaks its own language, and that it is not closely tied to specific words, is correct, and also appropriate in its praise of Rossini. For in his comic operas one has the strongest sense of all his characters being motivated by the same force, which is part of the farcical effect they create. And just as we saw Schopenhauer describing us as so many puppets on strings, so the figures in all farce, but Rossini's in particular, give the impression of approximating to automata, with the odd feeling thrown in. And the famous Rossini crescendo, especially in vocal ensembles, gives the sense of a group of people losing their identities as they become more animated, and ending up as a kind of blob of wilfulness.

Schopenhauer continues from the last passage:

As a result of all this, we can regard the phenomenal world, or nature, and music as two different expressions of the same thing; and this thing itself is therefore the only medium of their analogy, a knowledge of which is required if we are to understand that analogy. Accordingly music, if regarded as an expression of the world, is in the highest degree a universal language that is related to the universality of concepts much as these are related to the particular things.

This is a riddling passage, suggesting as it does that only through understanding the nature of the world shall we undersand the analogy between the phenomenal world and music. How, though, are we to understand the world itself, that is the will, except through some kind of representation? On this question Schopenhauer founders, I think. He is in the dilemma that confronts everyone who both maintains that there is in a deep sense only one thing, and that to know something is to be separate from it and to penetrate it with one or another form of understanding. For if there is only one thing, then there is no question of an externally placed understander coming to grips with it. If it is to be understood, it must come to grips with itself, and therefore at least have parts.

As he moves on from the joys of music, Schopenhauer envisages other ways in which we may seek what he rather fancifully calls 'salvation'. They involve progressively more drastic ways of renouncing the will-to-live, until one loses one's individuality altogether and achieves oneness – but with what? With, of course, the only thing that there really is: the will itself. Is that what we want to do, given his accounts of it? It is hard to see how we could. Erich Heller, in his commentary on Thomas Mann's great novel *Buddenbrooks*, seems to put the position with definitive brevity:

And what is the Will? We know the gloomy answer. And yet the eternal forms of this disastrous Will, when devoutly contemplated, lead the saint towards the ecstatic adoration of their creator, and the artist towards their imitation in works of art, the supreme pleasure of the human mind.

Arthur Schopenhauer (1788–1860) was born in Danzig. He was educated in France, England, Switzerland and Austria. Admiring Kant, he found his idealist successors, especially Hegel, appalling, and throughout his life loathed academic philosophers and their jargon. Attempting to rival Hegel by scheduling his lectures at the same time, he drew no audience and was further embittered. He was also a violent misogynist, and wrote scathingly on women. He lived in a secluded, sedentary style in Frankfurt, though he was a keen theatregoer. He went each morning to the public library to read *The Times*, which he regarded as the most reliable source of information on the world's miseries. During his last years his fame at last began to spread, though that did nothing to improve his temper. Among his most ardent disciples were Wagner and, for a time, Nietzsche.

Tanner, Michael.

Schopenhauer.

DATE			

BAKER & TAYLOR